From Grafton, *Six World War II Postcards,* a Dover Publications

954 NORTH AMERICAN B-25 MEDIUM BOMBER
KEEP 'EM
FLYING!
MARINE CORPS
NAVY
ARMY
Jusmeti

LET'S PULL TOGETHER
V4
V
(C) 1941 Tichnor Bros., Inc.
THE SOLDIER ★ THE SAILOR ★ AND YOU

From Grafton, *Six World War II Postcards,* a Dover Publications

From Grafton, *Six World War II Postcards*, a Dover Publications

SO WE'LL MEET AGAIN
BUY MORE WAR BONDS

OVER THE TOP
FOR VICTORY
V2
(C) 1941 Tichnor Bros., Inc.

From Grafton, *Six World War II Postcards,* a Dover Publications

From Grafton, *Six World War II Postcards,* a Dover Publications

Greetings from
WILL ROGERS
FIELD
OKLAHOMA

A. C.-3

Keep 'Em

Flying!

BOMBER

From Grafton, *Six World War II Postcards,* a Dover Publications